MYSTERY SHOPPING I

By Suzanne Hill

****

Hill Publishing Company

****

Published by: Hill Publishing, PO Box 76731, Colorado Springs, CO 80970-6731

Chapter 1

Mystery Shopping – How I Discovered It

I came across mystery shopping purely by accident and didn't believe that I could actually get paid to evaluate products and services and get stuff for free. That just did not seem possible to me so I decided to try it out for myself. I had a considerable amount of skepticism because I had tried a variety ways to make money by starting a variety of businesses and was always disappointed.

I tried it out and realized that I could get so many things for free. I found mystery shops for casual dining, quick service dining, fast food, convenience stores, grocery stores, drug stores, mass merchants, online stores, retail banks, insurance companies, investment companies, automotive dealers, automotive repair shops, oil change shops, medical practices, medical devices and products, dental visits, consumer products, airport and travel services, entertainment venues (such as, movie theaters, tourist attractions, theme parks), hotel stay, gambling at casinos, spa services, and so much more. I went to amusement parks, indoor skydiving, saw movies, went out to eat, got a designer items, went gambling, and went on vacations for free.

So I told a few friends and family members and they all wanted to know how I did it so I decided I would write a book. I really wish I had all of this information when I began because it would have made the process smoother. I learned how to mystery shop by doing it but it took some trial and error to find companies and the information I needed to succeed. This book provides that for you.

I decided I would write a book dedicated to mystery shopping so other people could learn how to do this too. I really wish I had all of this information when I began because it would have made the process smoother. I learned how to mystery shop by doing it but it took some trial and error to find companies and the information I needed to succeed. This book provides that for you.

Many people get into mystery shopping because it is fun. That is one of the main reasons I continued mystery shopping after I conducted my initial research. I love getting "free" stuff. I honestly think "FREE" is my favorite word. I also enjoy acting out scenarios and pretending. It is a lot of fun. It doesn't hurt that I get paid to do it. It is so fun to get paid to shop. I love that I get to choose which shops I will perform and can work as much or as little as I want. I was impressed that the reports submitted are taken very seriously and used to improve businesses. I have seen it first hand.

Both myself and my husband mystery shop. We both happened to be "mystery shopping" the same restaurant. I was scheduled to shop the restaurant on a Tuesday, and he was scheduled on Friday. I showed up and the restaurant was a disaster. There was ice all over the floor, the ice machines were out of ice, the soda machine was filthy, it took approximately 10 minutes before someone acknowledged me and they were not busy, and overall, everything was a disaster. I let my husband know what I encountered during my visit to the restaurant, so he was prepared when he went on Friday.

I prepared my report for the shop and turned it in. On Friday when my husband went to the location, he stated that the location was immaculate, there were two managers on site, and he was acknowledged and served within 10 seconds. This just shows the impact you can have as a mystery shopper. As you can see corporations take these reports very seriously.

I have studied business for many years and have always been interested in how businesses run and what makes then successful as far back as I can remember. Mystery shopping is a perfect fit for me because I love every aspect of it. When you love what you are doing it is not really a job, it is fun. I love seeing how businesses run and what makes them successful.

Mystery shopping is considered an at home business so there are many write-offs included in mystery shopping. So not only can you get things for free you can also write-off purchases and mileage on your taxes. There will be a section at the end of the book on how to do this. The current mileage rate is 57.5¢ per mile traveled for business. Each mystery shop is considered a business activity, as well as, any time you purchase items for your business. This includes things like a mileage book and a 3-ring binder to keep copies of all your receipts.

In the section on being an independent contractor, I will show you the system I use to keep track of all my expenses, earnings and mileage. I have a close friend who is a tax accountant and she helped me set up my first business with everything that I would need at tax time. When you have a system it makes it easier to find everything at tax time. It is also essential in case you are ever audited. This will allow you to show proof of all purchases, earnings and mileage if ever requested.

Chapter 2

Mystery Shopping Industry Overview

Mystery shopping began in the 1940s as a way for companies to see the customer service that their customers were receiving on a day-to-day basis. Mystery shopping measures quality of service, evaluates whether the organization is compliant with all safety and workplace regulations, and also gathers information about specific products and services. An organization can have a mystery shopper shop their company to see how they are performing, or a company can mystery shop the competition to see what other companies are providing that they are not.

Mystery shoppers are also hired sometimes by watchdog organizations to make sure companies are following the law and to document any unethical behavior. There are even occasions when a company will hire a mystery shopper to find out what different stores think about their product.

Organizations hire mystery shoppers so they can truly find out what is happening at the different locations they have. When a company knows that their headquarters is coming to inspect, they clean everything up nice and neat. They are also on their best behavior. I have been through many of these "inspections" and the inspectors never get the real picture of how their company is operating. This also prevents the company from seeing what type of service is provided on a day-to-day basis.

There are numerous benefits to hiring mystery shoppers to determine the customer service the average customer gets. First, when a customer anonymously enters a store, the employees are not aware that this customer is evaluating them because they blend in with all the other customers. Second, when companies know that they are being mystery shopped then they are "on their toes" so to speak. The employees make sure that they are following procedures all the time because they never know who the "mystery" shopper is. When you conduct mystery shops for organizations you are required to sign a non-disclosure agreement (NDA) to ensure that all of the trade secrets for the company you are completing the shop for are kept confidential. This is very important because you are privy to confidential company information which you use to evaluate the organization.

Mystery shopping is used by a variety of organizations. The following are organizations that use mystery shoppers, but this list is not all inclusive:

- Retailers of all types - Grocery Stores, Convenience Stores, Clothing Stores, Department Stores, Sports Equipment Stores, etc.
- Fast Casual Restaurants

- Fine Dining Restaurants
- Bars/Clubs
- Bowling Alleys
- Cell Phone Service Providers
- Carpet Cleaners
- Car Rental Agencies
- Casinos
- Coffee Shops
- Day Cares
- Copy & Print Shops
- Delivery Services
- Dry Cleaners
- Florists
- Funeral Homes
- Gift Shops
- Government Agencies
- Financial Institutions
- Home Builders
- Automotive Sales and Service
- Motorcycle/Car Dealers
- Marinas
- Health Clubs
- Airlines

- Nursing Homes
- Online Services
- RV Parks
- Travel Companies
- Self-Storage Facilities
- Truck & Trailer Rental
- Truck Stops
- Dentists
- Vision Care Providers
- Physicians
- Theme Parks, Museums, Theaters, etc.
- Professional and Amateur Sports
- Government Agencies (i.e., DOT)
- Insurance Companies
- Apartment Communities
- Healthcare Companies & Facilities
- Hotels, Resorts, & Timeshares
- Spas
- Hair Salons
- Municipal Government (Libraries, Parks)
- Educational Institutions
- Gaming Industries
- Marijuana Shops

- Churches
- Strip Clubs
- And Many Others

Mystery shopping is used by pretty much every industry that has interactions with customers. Companies have a sizable investment in market research which insures their continued growth and success. Mystery shopping verifies that company policies are being properly implemented, that employees are performing up to par and being productive, that brand identity is being properly promoted, it uncovers any disconnect with company mission or vision, verifies that there are enough employees working to meet the demand, and determines if any additional training is required at various locations.

Mystery shopping is not about giving your opinion of the location. It is about describing exactly what you see. You are providing the facts of the situation. One of the key traits of a mystery shopper is being highly observant. Mystery shoppers document their observations and answer questions regarding these observations. This information helps ensure that companies are serving their customers with the best customer service. Customer frustration leads to the following: 13% tell 15 or more people if they're unhappy. Conversely 72% of consumers will share a positive experience with 6 or more people. So now you can see why these results are so important to companies.

For a company to have a successful mystery shopping program, they need to have thousands of mystery shoppers. They need thousands of people to shop at all of their locations to get a true picture of the service being provided. The average company has about 5,000 mystery shops a month conducted to get an accurate picture of the customer service provided.

Companies also need diversity in their mystery shoppers so they can see if there is any difference in service provided to each ethnic group. Companies want to make sure all of their customers are receiving equal treatment regarding ethnicity, age, location, and socioeconomic factors.

As a mystery shopper you are classified as an independent contractor. This means you do not work directly for the mystery shopping company. You are contracted to complete each mystery shop. This means you are not eligible for benefits or workman's compensation. Mystery shopping is a business. This also gives you immense flexibility to work for more than one company and to work whenever you want.

More than half, 63% of mystery shoppers work for 3 or more mystery shopping companies. 53% of mystery shoppers have been working as mystery shopping independent contractors for 3 or more years. Mystery shoppers typically shop for an average of 3.75 different industries. When companies can hire independent contractors to perform mystery shops, they can pay higher fees because they do not have the administrative costs associated with an employee position.

Most mystery shoppers conduct shops on a part-time basis. There are some mystery shoppers that do mystery shopping on a full-time basis, but the percentage is much lower. This business allows you to pick and choose the shops that you will take and work when you want with no fear of losing your independent contractor status.

The type of shops that people take is a personal preference. Some people take shops based on what they are looking to buy or what they currently need now. For example, if it is time for you to get your oil changed or you need car maintenance you can take a shop for that. You may want to go to a movie or amusement park and choose to do a shop for that. There are numerous options available and the shops you take are a personal preference.

The results you enter on your report are consolidated with all the mystery shops completed at that specific location during the month by the company to get an overall picture as to how their company is performing overall. Completing a mystery shop report is about answering questions and writing narratives about your observations.

There is a myth regarding mystery shoppers stating that they "shop" just to write bad reports about employees and get them in trouble. This is not the case. Mystery shop reports have a series of questions that must be answered yes or no. When a requirement has been met and you answer yes there are no comments "generally" required. When a requirement has not been met a comment is required to explain the reasons the requirement was not met. In some instances, depending on the shop, a picture may also be required if the requirement has not been met. When a requirement hasn't been met it takes more time for the shopper to complete the report.

According to The State of Customer Experience (2012), 93% of companies have improving the customer experience as a top priority of their organization. The State of Customer Experience (2012) also stated that 75% of companies aim to differentiate themselves based on customer service. Mystery shopping is a tool for companies to ensure that their operational policies are being properly implemented. The data garnered from mystery shops reports is used to ensure business growth and increased productivity.

Mystery shoppers do not decide if the experience they had was good or bad, they just evaluate whether the employee met the standards set forth by the employer. When the employer receives the report, they decide how they will use the information. Most companies use the reports to coach employees on how to improve their customer service skills and do a better job moving forward.

A mystery shop report is a tool used by organizations to determine their strengths and weaknesses. Honesty is paramount when you are completing and submitting these reports because in some instances an organization will review its video footage to corroborate the report they received. Submitting a false report can lead to the termination of your independent contractor status with a mystery shopping company.

Each mystery company has editors that review your shop report prior to sending it to the company. When the editor reviews your shop report, they look for excellent grammar, complete sentences, correct spelling, no opinions listed in the report unless specifically asked for, assurance that all questions in the report have been answered, and assurance that all shop requirements have been met. Each report is graded. Most companies grade your report on a scale from 1-10, some grade on a scale of 1-100, and there are also some other variations.

The ability to get awarded certain shops is based on a variety of factors. One factor is the average report rating of the shops you have submitted. Most shops have a requirement that your report average must be within a certain range, such as 8-10, to be able to accept the shop. There are other qualifications too that are sometimes listed. These include requirements that you have not shopped the location in the last 30 days, that you have a Gold certification from the MSPA, that you have completed a certification required to perform the shop, and other various qualifications. That is why it is so important to read the shop before you take it to make sure you meet all the qualifications listed.

Mystery shopping companies have these qualifications for certain shops to ensure that a qualified, experienced mystery shopper is assigned to the shop. With some mystery shopping companies, you are limited in the amount of shops that you can accept until you reach a certain level. This is to show that you are reliable and that you turn in good quality reports on time. The higher end shops are normally given to mystery shoppers who have a Gold Certification from MSPA and have an average mystery shop report rating on the high end of the scale, such as an average between 8 and 10.

These high end/brand name shops include things like high end purses, watches, clothing, etc. A mystery shopping company who is doing a client shop must ensure the shopper they hire is reliable and will provide accurate information. Mystery shopping companies depend on mystery shoppers to provide excellent, quality reports. Mystery shopping companies provide this quality information to the client. Mystery shopping companies keep contracts with an organization by providing overall excellent data on time to show the strengths and weaknesses of the organization.

Editors will review your report prior to it being submitted to the client to ensure accuracy. If an incomplete or inaccurate report is submitted, your shop will be invalidated, and it will be given to another mystery shopper. When this happens, you do not get paid and you receive a 0 grade on your report. This brings your average down and may prevent you from being awarded shops in the future.

Chapter 3

Mystery Shopping Providers Association (MSPA)

The Mystery Shopping Providers Association (MSPA) is an organization that has both mystery shoppers and Mystery Shopping companies as members. The MSPA helps to connect companies with mystery shoppers to conduct shops. This is a beneficial relationship for all involved. The MSPA also helps to protect the industry, provides various certifications, informs its members of scams, and overall brings validity to the industry.

This global organization aims to promote the mystery shopping industry in a positive light by improving service and promoting excellence. They do this by providing training and certifications to mystery shoppers. They also have an area on their website where they inform their members of any current scams that have been occurring in the industry. They provide a description of the scams and what to look out for. The MSPA overall ensures professionalism in the industry and ensures mystery shopping companies receive quality data and reports. The website for the MSPA is http://www.mspa-global.org/ I would highly recommend becoming a member of the MSPA because they offer and provide a tremendous amount of value.

They also advise their members of the different regulations in each country through provided training. An example of a difference in country regulations is in the United States you are often asked to get the description of an employee and their name. In Europe, however, they have very strict privacy laws and they do not require this, to protect their citizen's privacy.

Mystery shopping includes recording how employees perform a specific set of standards. Mystery shoppers also ensure proper placement of products, conduct price checks, conduct consumer product placements, verify store traffic patterns, inquire as to the opinion's employees hold about certain products, and many other variations. The MSPA does have guidelines that their mystery shopping companies must follow to be a member of the MSPA. These mystery shopping companies cannot use mystery shopping reports as a sole reason to reprimand or fire an employee. Mystery shopping reports can be used as a source to retrain employees on proper procedures to increase customer satisfaction and customer loyalty. They must also agree to conduct mystery shops only within the letter of the law. A mystery shop cannot be done if it breaks the law.

The number of mystery shops a company requests to be conducted on a monthly basis varies widely by the size of the organization, the number of employees an organization has, and the requirement for an organization to create a truly representative sample. A sample is a subset of a population. A representative sample is one that is chosen so that its characteristics are similar to that of the population. A representative sample is a selected segment of a group that closely parallels the population in terms of the key variables under examination. This is one of the main reasons mystery shopping companies ask you to fill out the demographic location of an application for the company. Each mystery shopping company wants to make sure they have a representative sample that is representative of the customers they serve.

Mystery shops are generally scheduled on different days of the weeks and at different times to get a sample of what customer service is like at different times of the day and week. This variety also provides a more representative sample of what their customers experience on a daily basis. Companies like a representative sample so they can truly see what customer service is being provided and how that customer service varies over time.

Chapter 4

Types of Mystery Shops

Traditional Mystery Shop – A traditional mystery shop includes posing as a real customer and evaluating the customer service received. This evaluation is conducted by completing an evaluation that includes a series of questions and written narratives that you are required to write to fully explain in detail what you observed. You provide a narrative which generally includes cleanliness of the location, sales skills of the employees, and the customer service received during the visit.

Reveal Shop – A reveal shop has an award component to it. A reveal shop is a lot like a traditional mystery shop but when an employee meets certain criteria you can provide a reward to the employee. These awards are generally things like awards or gift certificates. One example would be a shop I had at an amusement park and there was a reveal portion at the end of the shop. I was able to provide one employee with an award and a gift certificate for the employee I felt went above and beyond to provide excellent customer service. These shops are a lot of fun because you get to make someone's day by giving them an award and recognition in front of their co-workers.

Competitive Shop – A competitive shop is where you compare multiple locations. The comparison could be for customer service at the different locations of a chain business or it could be multiple businesses with a comparison of a certain product. I have done many of these shops. You fill out the same form at each location so an organization can compare the similarities and differences between locations.

You will see these often for cell phone shops. A manufacturer of a specific phone brand will hire mystery shoppers to determine what local cell phone companies say about their product. For example, if XYZ Cell Phone Company wants to find out what each cell phone company and store is saying about their new XYZ phone they would do a comparison shop. They would send you to the big cell phone providers and local technology stores to see what employee opinions are regarding the new phone.

Pricing Audit – A pricing audit is a little bit different than a traditional mystery shop. During a pricing audit, a mystery shopper enters a location and discreetly notes the prices of certain items. This can be accomplished as a competitive shop or an audit. During a competitive shop you discreetly note prices at a variety of locations so the organization can see the difference between prices at different locations. During an audit you would discreetly document prices at just one location. Some pricing audits require you to discreetly take a picture of the menu with the prices listed or a menu board in a fast-food restaurant to get a picture of the prices.

Telephone Shops – There are a few different variations of the telephone shop. The telephone shop could be done by itself or as part of a traditional mystery shop. The shop generally has a report that is filled out and goes to the client. The call may be recorded and given to the client. This may be in addition to the report or in some rare instances the client will just receive the recording.

Audio & Video Shops – When you conduct and audio or video shop, you record the entire shop. There are many intricacies with video and audio shops. You must ensure that you are following the laws with regard to recording in the area you are in. Before conducting a video or audio shop, you should practice. You use a hidden camera to record the interaction. Practicing is important because you need to ensure that the camera is pointed in the right direction and there are no obstructions in front of the camera. You could use a buttonhole camera or a pen camera. There are numerous different types of hidden cameras. You must also practice with an audio recording. You need to make sure the recording is clear and that there is not interference, such as, the audio recorder rubbing up against something or being muffled.

I would suggest taking the training offered by the MSPA Video Shopping I and Video Shopping II if you plan on conducting hidden video mystery shops. The Video Shopping I course covers the basics of conducting video mystery shops. The training covers the basics of how to use a hidden video camera, what the client expects during a hidden video shop, the normal errors that occur while conducting these shops, and the laws with regard to conducting these shops. The Video Shopping II course is a hands-on training. You role play and experiment with hidden video equipment to learn how to successfully use the equipment. You receive feedback and helpful hints from the instructor on the use of the equipment. You have to submit a sample video shop to the MSPA in order to receive your certification.

Digital Photo Shops – These shops are generally part of a traditional mystery shop. You take digital photos discreetly, so the employees do not know you are taking the pictures. I found that the best way to do that is with your smart phone. People look at their phones all the time, so it does not look suspicious. Make sure the flash is off before you take the picture, so you are not discovered.

Internet Service Evaluation – There are a few variations of the internet shop. You could be asked to purchase an item to determine how the delivery process works and the customer service you receive. You may either be required to have to order directly shipped to you or shipped to a local store and then be required to pick it up. You may be allowed to keep the item or may be required to return it. Make sure you read the instructions, so you meet all requirements.

Another variation would be to conduct a shop where you email customer services or technical support and see how long it takes them to respond. The company is also looking for the type of response you receive and if the response is proper based on company guidelines.

Another variation is where you would be asked to sign up for an online account to beta test a new customer system to see how user friendly the system is and whether the payment feature works properly. I recently did a shop to test our local utilities company new payment system. On this particular shop, they paid the bill for you if you signed up for their new payment system to ensure there are no glitches before they roll it out to all customers. A company does not want to roll out a new system to their customers and then realize there are serious issues with the system. They would rather pay a small group of beta testers to ensure the system works before rolling it out and upsetting their customers.

Integrity Shops – This is a shop where you observe an employee to ensure they are being honest. This may include how they handle cash or provide a service, such as, bartending. There are a considerable amount of integrity checks in bars to ensure that bartenders are properly handling cash and not over pouring alcohol. Bars lose a considerable amount of money through over pouring, free drinks, and improperly handled cash.

When you do an integrity shop you have specific instructions that must be followed exactly. For example, you may be required to buy two drinks and pay for one with cash and one with a credit card. You generally must report what time you bought the drink so they can check receipts to ensure everything was entered in the register. You normally watch closely as to what the bartender does with the cash you give him for drink. Generally, you also watch the bartender pour drinks for a specific amount of time and record the drinks bought. You record what was ordered and what was given to the customer. For example, someone could order a single and be given a double and this would be something that must be notated.

Government agencies conduct shops to ensure that regulations are being followed. An example of a government agency conducting a shop to determine that the proper procedures are being followed when conducting drug tests on future and current employees. These integrity shops are important because if a lab is allowing people to cheat on drug tests it destroys the integrity of drug testing.

Trade associations also conduct mystery shops to ensure that their credentials are being properly used. I did a mystery shop for an association who wanted to check and see if a former member was using their credentials after leaving the organization and no longer paying membership fees. This type of shop includes going to the location and checking to see if any certification paperwork is posted or referenced. You generally also conduct a full search of the business' website to check for certification reference or posting. You would generally take pictures of the certifications posted and screenshots from the website and include them with the report.

Chapter 5

Mystery Shopper Qualifications

A mystery shopper can be anyone who is 18 years of age or older. Companies hire mystery shoppers that are representative of the demographic profiles of their customers. To meet this qualification, mystery shopping companies hire a variety of people from all walks of life. When you submit your application to a mystery shopping company there is a section on demographics included. They ask for things like race, age, annual income, languages you speak, locations you frequent, and a variety of other questions. These demographics are very important because they help the mystery shopping company decide who is best suited to conduct a shop based on the qualifications of the client.

There are no particular educational requirements or experience needed to become a mystery shopper. Some mystery shopping companies prefer shoppers with experience and certifications. Some companies give preference to shoppers who have experience in the industry they are shopping in because of specialized knowledge. You cannot shop for a company (client) where you previously worked in most cases. You also cannot shop for any companies (clients) your immediate family is currently working for or has worked for in the past, in most cases. This is due to the fact these instances can cause a conflict of interest.

Certification through the MSPA is not required but it is preferred by many companies. The certifications offered by the MSPA help you gain the skills necessary to successfully conduct mystery shops. These certifications also show you are committed to be a professional mystery shopper.

The certifications offered by MSPA require membership in order to take these trainings. Certification programs allow you to make informed decisions and professional improvements for yourself and your industry. The MSPA offers eleven different certifications in the mystery shopping industry. The certifications offered are Intro to Mystery Shopping (previously called the Silver Certification), Gold Certification, Professional Responsibility and Ethics, Professional Report Writing, Quick Service Restaurant and Casual Dining, Fine Dining,

Banking & Financial Institutions I, Brands Standard Auditing, Retail I, Video Shopping I and Video Shopping II.

The Intro to Mystery Shopping course which was formerly known as the Silver Certification is an overview of the mystery shopping industry. When filling out applications for mystery shopping companies they still ask for your Silver Certification code not the Intro to Mystery Shopping code to show you have this certification. This course covers the basic practices and required skills that are necessary to be a mystery shopper. This course is the prerequisite to the take the other offered courses.

The Gold Certification course is an advanced level introductory course. This is the certification that is coveted by many mystery shopping companies. Mystery shopping companies tend to give high end and coveted shops to those shoppers who have the Gold Certification. They do this because people who take the Gold Certification course truly want to be professional mystery shoppers and take this position seriously.

The course teaches the advanced skills needed to be an expert mystery shopper. The Gold Certification course includes a section on how to successfully write a narrative of a mystery shop. This is an essential skill to learn when conducting mystery shops. When I completed this certification course several years ago it was offered on DVD. They have changed this effective September 2017 and you now receive a link to the videos. This makes the process easier because you do not have to wait to receive the DVD's in the mail.

The Professional Responsibility and Ethics course teaches you how to properly set up your mystery shopping business. The course also teaches the legal and industry accepted standards of the mystery shopping industry. It goes over the ethics that are expected by all in the industry. The reports written are essential to helping companies improve their customer service and their accurateness affects many people. This is why accuracy is so paramount.

The Professional Industry Writing course teaches how to write a well-written and descriptive report. A well-written and descriptive report is the key to a successful mystery shop. Vocabulary, grammar, spelling, and proper writing skills are essential to an excellent report.

Proper writing skills are important because the way you word a sentence can describe precisely what you see and gives an exact impression. Here are two sentences and you can see how one describes the situation better than the other. I walked into the room and it was messy. I walked in the room and there were books, magazines, and clothes strewn all over the floor and dirty dishes on the coffee table. You can see that the second sentence clearly provides a better description of what was observed in the room.

Mystery shopping companies are looking to hire mystery shoppers who submit the best reports that need the least amount of editing. When reports do not need additional editing, it saves the mystery shopping company money because of reduced editing and proofreading time. Schedulers prefer to give shops to those shoppers that provide highly rated reports because this causes less rework. Editors and proofreaders spend the bulk of their time fixing the same typical errors: generic writing, improper choice of vocabulary and inconsistency in writing. Schedulers work closely with the editors and want to make their jobs as easy as possible.

The Quick Service Restaurant and Casual Dining course explains and teaches how to conduct quick service restaurant and casual dining shops. These types of shops are the most common shops in the mystery shopping industry. The forms that are required for these shops are rather simple and usually do not require extensive narratives. They do however require timings, discreet pictures to be taken, and a clear, concise description of what was observed. There can be multiple timings required during these shops which can be complicated.

The Fine Dining course is more complex in that fine dining mystery shops require excellent concentration and observation, excellent note taking skills, and the ability to blend in with the clientele of the restaurant. These shops are normally given to the most experienced and trustworthy mystery shoppers because these reports require lengthy comments in multiple sections. During these shops you generally interact with six or seven employees and must keep accurate notes of each interaction. Excellent writing skills are imperative with fine dining shops. The course teaches you the ins and outs of fine dining and how to write concise, sequential narratives.

The Banking & Financial Institutions I course teaches the high level of sales and service standards of the industry. The financial industry requires strict governmental compliance because of the finance laws and regulations. The banking and finance industry must ensure that they have compliance with these laws and regulations, so they depend on mystery shoppers to ensure they are complaint.

The Brands Standard Auditing course teaches brand auditing. A brand audit is where you announce that you are doing an audit as soon as you enter the location. These types of audits ensure compliance with the mandatory brand standards the company expects to be in place. The course gives an overview of the industry, the requirements needed to be a successful auditor, and how to find auditing work.

The Retail I course is a general overview of the retail industry. The course includes the history of the retail industry, terminology used in the industry, and an explanation of the common shops types in the retail industry. This course also explains how to make accurate observations and properly record them in your shop report.

Video Shopping I and Video Shopping II are important to take if you plan on conducting hidden video mystery shops. The Video Shopping I course covers the basics of conducting video mystery shops. The training covers the basics of how to use a hidden video camera, what the client expects during a hidden video shop, the normal errors that occur while conducting these shops, and the laws with regard to conducting these shops.

The Video Shopping II course is a hands-on training. You role play and experiment with hidden video equipment to learn how to successfully use the equipment. You receive feedback and helpful hints from the instructor on the use of the equipment. You have to submit a sample video shop to the MSPA in order to receive your certification.

There are some very important traits you must possess as a mystery shopper. I would say the most important trait you need to possess is to be reliable. That trait would be closely followed by being organized.

The biggest problem in the mystery shopping industry is shoppers not being reliable. Schedulers have a difficult job because they must make sure that each shop required by the client is scheduled and completed. When a shopper doesn't follow through with a scheduled shop the scheduler has to reschedule the shop with another shopper. They call this a "flake" in the mystery shopping industry. "Flake" is defined when a shopper doesn't do a shop and doesn't communicate that fact to the mystery shopping. This happens approximately 25% of the time.

This causes a huge problem for the mystery shopping company as they have to find someone quickly to complete the shop to meet the client's deadline. In most cases, the mystery shopping company will offer a bonus to get it completed by the deadline. If you have a flexible schedule you can make extra money by completing these last-minute shops.

Organization is also extremely important because you will be juggling multiple timelines and requirements. It is essential to read the shop requirements prior to completing the shop to ensure all the requirements are met and nothing has been missed. I know I have said this numerous times but this is an essential step in being a mystery shopper. There can be multiple components to a shop that must be completed on multiple days, so organization is the key to success.

There are some shops that require more than one person to complete the shop. When you conduct a dinner shop, it generally requires two people. There are shops to tourist attractions and amusement parks that can have larger group requirements. I have been on an amusement park shop which was for six people. These shops sometimes include groups because families or large groups are the company's demographic.

The things you need to successful in mystery shopping are reliable internet access, a cell phone (smart phone), digital camera (I use the camera on my cell phone), video recording equipment, scanner, stopwatch, digital recorder, and phone recorder. Some people use their cell phone for most of these requirements. Smart phones can be used to access the internet, take digital photos, as a stopwatch, and to scan and upload documents.

Chapter 6

Being an Independent Contractor

The IRS explains that you are generally self-employed if you have a trade or business as a sole proprietor or independent contractor, you are a member of a partnership that has a business or a trade, or you are in business for yourself. A mystery shopper works as an independent contractor for mystery shopping companies. So as an independent contractor you are self-employed in the eyes of the IRS.

Since mystery shopping is a business it is important to keep track of your purchases, income, and mileage. All of these are important when you file your taxes at the end of the year. You will file a Schedule C in the United States. Taxes vary by country. The purchases you make, and your mileage are tax deductions from your income, in general.

I have set up an accounting system to keep track of all of these items for our taxes. I use a three-ring binder with sheet protectors to keep my receipts and all the payments I have received for the year. I have two sections in the three-ring binder; one section for any fees or reimbursements received from mystery shopping companies and one section for my expenses. I tape each receipt to a piece of paper and below the receipt I write the date, location of purchase, what was purchased, and the amount. I do this because over time receipts can fade and in this instance, you need to know what the receipt was for when filing your taxes.

It is very important to keep all of your receipts. You may not only have to submit a copy with your mystery shopping report, but you will also need it for tax purposes. There are certain things you will not be able to get a receipt for. In these instances, make a note of the expense, date, time, and purpose of the expense.

This can happen if you need to put money in a parking meter to conduct a shop. The parking meter may not give you a receipt. You would write down the date, time, amount paid for the parking meter, and the shop you are conducting which required the expense. When this occurs, it is essential to make a note so you have a written record. It is imperative to get a receipt whenever possible.

At the end of the year you will add up all of the expenses you had during the year and deduct these expenses from your earnings. I suggest getting a tax professional's help to complete your taxes. You must figure your net profit or net loss from your business. You do this by subtracting your business expenses from your business income. If your expenses are less than your income, the difference is net profit and becomes part of your income. If your expenses are more than your income, the difference is a net loss. You usually can deduct your loss from gross income.

There are many mystery shops around tax time that allow you to get the cost of getting your taxes done by a professional reimbursed. Whether you take a mystery shop or not, I suggest you get a tax professional to assist you in filing your taxes. This help will probably dramatically increase the amount of your tax return.

It is essential to keep all receipts, documents of payments received, and mileage logs if you ever get audited. In the United States, the IRS will audit up to 3 tax years back. I have a mileage log where I keep track of all my mileage because this is also a tax-deductible expense. In the mileage log I write down the name and address of the location, reason I went, the date, and the total mileage for the trip.

Here is an example:

Name & Address of Location	Date	Total Mileage	Reason for Trip
Oil Change Company 123 Main St., Colorado Springs, CO 80916	1/1/18	18	Oil Change Shop
Office Supply Store 123 Main St., Colorado Springs, CO 80916	1/2/18	22	Purchase Office Supplies from Office Supply Store
Restaurant 123 Main St., Colorado Springs, CO 80916	1/3/18	13	Restaurant Shop
Total Mileage for the Month		**53**	

There are expenses that are tax deductible as an independent contractor. These expenses include supplies, mileage, cell phone cost (% used for business), internet cost (% used for business), banking fees, business travel, education/training (for profession), office supplies, postage, dues for professional organizations (like the MSPA), equipment needed for your profession, equipment repair, and other various business-related costs.

If you use part of your home for business, you may be able to deduct expenses for the business use of your home. The home office deduction is available for homeowners and renters and applies to all types of homes. To be deductible, a business expense must be both ordinary and necessary.

An ordinary expense is one that is common and accepted in your trade or business. A necessary expense is one that is helpful and appropriate for your trade or business. An expense does not have to be indispensable to be considered necessary.

When working as an independent contractor, mystery shopping companies do not take taxes out of your income. You are responsible for paying taxes on the income you earn. That is why it is essential to keep good records. You can deduct your expenses from your income which lowers your overall tax burden.

You are also responsible for paying self-employment tax as an independent contractor. Self-employment taxes include Social Security and Medicare. You will complete a Schedule SE to pay these self-employment taxes. It is similar to the Social Security and Medicare taxes withheld from the pay of most wage earners. In general, anytime the wording "self-employment tax" is used; it only refers to Social Security and Medicare taxes and not any other tax (like income tax). A 1040 ES is filed quarterly to pay self-employment taxes. These quarterly filings are due on January 15th, April 15th, June 15th, and September 15th.

In the United States, if a company pays you more than $600 in a year, they must issue you a 1099 which shows the income you received from the company. When you work for a company and make less than $600 a year you do not receive a 1099 but you must still report your income. The IRS receives information on payments made by companies even if you do not receive a 1099. It is imperative to claim all of the income you received during the year. You never want to be on the bad side of the IRS.

You never want to be audited but if you are unfortunately the subject of an IRS audit it is essential to have all your documentation to prove your income, expenses, and mileage. I have a service where I have hired a lawyer to answer any questions I have regarding my business and this service also provides a tax attorney to accompany you during an audit. If you are interested in this service send me an email at suzanne_marie_hill@yahoo.com and I will send you information on this service. The cost is very reasonable (less than $30 a month).

There are benefits to working as an independent contractor. As an independent contractor you can work for more than one company and work whenever you want. This means you can choose the mystery shopping jobs you want to take. You have great flexibility as an independent contractor.

The Independent Contractor Agreement (ICA) you sign with each mystery shopping company has a Non-Disclosure Agreement (NDA) clause that prevents you from disclosing confidential information. As a mystery shopper you will learn the trade secrets of companies and these cannot be disclosed. The ICA also includes the fees you are paid for conducting mystery shops, the guidelines you must follow, any restrictions when conducting the shop, details on how to write your report after conducting the shop, and other pertinent information. The NDA applies not only to the company you are conducting the shop for but also to the proprietary information you learn about the mystery shopping company.

This does not mean that you cannot tell people you know that you conduct mystery shops in general, but you cannot divulge specifics. You cannot give proprietary information about the operating policies of companies, which mystery shopping companies shop which companies, or any other confidential information. It is also important to never post information about specifics on social media. You will be found out and lose your ability to mystery shop. Confidentiality is paramount in the mystery shopping industry.

Chapter 7

Mystery Shopping Scams

There are some scams out there so it is important to work with companies that are members of the Mystery Shopping Professionals Association (MSPA) or companies that you thoroughly vet. The MSPA helps to regulate the industry and provides its members with current mystery shop openings, a list of mystery shopping companies, a list of all the recent scams that are occuring in the industry, and training. The website for the MSPA is http://www.mspa-global.org/. I would highly recommend becoming a member of the MSPA because they offer a tremendous amout of value.

Scams are common and successful in the mystery shopping industry because many people do not know how the industry works. A real mystery shopping company will never charge you a fee to sign up with their company. A real mystery shopping company will also never send you a check and have you send them money back. Authentic mystery shopping companies never charge a fee and they pay you, not the other way around.

Scams are common in our industry and new twists on the classic check scam are developed every day. Scammers often operate by pretending to be MSPA members or mystery shopping companies. They contact the general public by email, telephone, job boards, or social media sites. They use fake names and titles to entice people to receive a check in the mail, conduct a false assignment, and then wire money or send items to a specified address. Regardless of the variations of this classic scam, the checks will bounce, and the victim is left footing the full bill and the bank fees associated with it.

You can find current scams listed on the MSPA website. Here are some examples of scams that have occurred in the industry:

- Confirm with Us, HS Brands, and IntelliShop are being impersonated by a scammer sending out fake checks with each company's name and logo. Do not cash these checks as they are fake, and you will have to pay considerable fees to your bank.
- There are emails being sent out by a scammer named Chris Nicholson posing as an employee for a

company called Consumer Delight Evaluations. The email address being used is eaxil32@gmail.com. Mystery shopping companies do not use generic email accounts. They use an email address that comes from the company they work for.

- There are scammers posing as MSPA representatives who are attempting to hire people for mystery shops. They are sending out fake checks. The MSPA does not hire or assign shoppers to shops. They are an association that links companies and shoppers but will NEVER hire or assign a shopper.

- QSI Specialists has been targeted by a scammer, their name and logo are being used in an ongoing scam using www.qsispecialistsLTD.com rather than their domain, www.qsispecialists.com.

- Dynamic Advantage has a scammer that created a very convincing webpage in order to impersonate them: http://www.da-shoppers.com/. The phone number and address on this page are incorrect while everything else looks like their actual website: http://dynamic-advantage.com/

- There is a scammer mailing letters from Helion Research that includes a fake check, instructions, and a survey. Mystery shopping companies do not send out mail to shoppers.
- Blink Research has been the target of a scammer who created a fake duplicate website at https://blinkserviceevaluators.com. There real website is https://blinkresearch.com.
- There are multiple scammer websites using the Secret Shopper logo. One is https://www.1secretshopper.com and another is http://undercover-shopper.com/. These two websites are unaffiliated with Secret Shopper. The real website is https://www.secretshopper.com.
- Helion Research has a scammer sending emails from info@job-helionresearch.com about an "evaluation exercise" that is another variation of the standard check scam. True emails from Helion will be from the @helionresearch.com domain.
- An email that appears to come from Liam Olivia at mjudisch@uiowa.edu that is said to represent the University of Iowa for a Mystery Shopping

Company is most definitely not a legitimate mystery shopping assignment.

- It is highly unlikely for a scheduler to first contact you via text! Reports have come in about a scammer texting from 304-449-6805. You will sometimes receive texts from schedulers, but this is a feature that you sign up for. You will not receive unrequested texts from mystery shopping companies.

- There have been reports that Carlton Robertson with Mystery Evaluations is contacting mystery shoppers. This appears to be an unfamiliar company. The communication from Mystery Evaluations comes from an email address info@mysteryevalutations.com and this does not seem to be a legitimate company.

- Anonymous Insights shared that a person by the name of Rebekah Patrick is attempting to steal their identity. She is representing herself as an employee of Anonymous Insights. She has created a Linked In profile that says that she has worked for Anonymous Insights since 2000 and gives an email address that follows the same format as Anonymous Insights (rpatrick@a-insights.com). This is not a real email address but if you reply to it, it will be sent to a different email address that is "hidden" behind it. THIS IS A SCAM. This person does not work for or represent Anonymous Insights, Inc. in any way. If you hear from her do not give her any personal information and do not accept anything from her. Report her to the police and BBB immediately.

- MSPA Headquarters has received numerous reports of messages being sent from MSPA staff looking to hiring evaluators. Since MSPA staff do not hire, we know this to be a scam.

- Don't be tricked by a company going by the name "Circle of Services." Circle of Services seems to be a typical check scammer.

- From Circle of Service: It seems that there is a group out there that has attached themselves to the Circle of Service logo and information. They are falsely sending mystery shopping opportunities to large groups of people on LinkedIn.

- Recently received from a shopper: I am Michael Richardson Recruitment Specialist with Sights On Service Inc. "We have a mystery shopping assignment in your area, and we would like you to participate." Secret Shopper® has been in business since 1990. We are a charter member of the Mystery Shopping Provider's Association (MSPA), the professional trade association for the Mystery Shopping industry. This is a scam!

- ABO Skin Serum, producer of Calypso, has been removing funds from people's accounts without sending them a product.

- Packages have been received by numerous mystery shoppers from a company called Mystery Guests Co. which included an assignment and a check for more than $3,000. This is a scam!

- Bestmark shared that someone has been masking their email as marketing@bestmark.com to conduct a phishing scam. Reply emails go to Eric Jennings at jenningsgroupllc@outlook.com and the scammer is offering $500 per shop, after asking for personal details. DO NOT REPLY!! Phishing is when a malicious party sends a fraudulent email disguised as a legitimate email, often purporting to be from a trusted source. The message is meant to trick the recipient into installing malware on his or her computer device or sharing personal or financial information.

Typing the website address into the address bar directly is the recommended approach to access a legitimate website and not a phishing site that was designed to mimic the real thing.

- A Shopper shared this on Facebook after receiving a bogus email: Gap Buster Inc is currently hiring for "Part Time Mystery Shoppers." Pay is $200/ weekly. If you are still interested, Kindly e-mail the following to: application@gapbusterinc.com. An email that came directly from GAP buster Worldwide would come from an email address with the ending @gbw.solutions/.

You will not receive emails from mystery shopping companies asking you to be a mystery shopper with an amount of pay listed. You may receive an email asking you to apply for a certain mystery shopping company as they need shoppers in your area. This will happen because another evaluator has shared your information and recommended you or they found your profile on the MSPA website. The email will let you know how they received your information. They will generally say they saw your profile on the MSPA website and are looking for a certified Gold shopper in your area.

When you encounter any scam, it is important to report them so scammers can be stopped and prosecuted. Scams can be reported to:

The Federal Trade Commission

https://www.ftccomplaintassistant.gov/

Internet Crime Compliant Center (IC3)

http://www.ic3.gov

State Attorney General's Office

http://www.naag.or/naag/attorneys-general/whos-my-ag.php

United States Postal Service (USPS) – If scam included something sent through the mail.

http://ehome.uspis.gov/fcsexternal/default.aspx

Mystery Shopper Providers Association (MSPA) – They will list scams that include member mystery shopping companies.

http://www.mspa-global.org/

The Better Business Bureau

https://www.bbb.org/consumer-complaints/file-a-complaint/get-started

Chapter 8

Mystery Shopping & Scheduling Companies

360 Intel

https://360intel.com

About Face

https://aboutfacecorp.com/shopper-pathway/shopper-login-page/

Ace Mystery Shopping

https://www.acemysteryshopping.com

Activa Research

https://www.activaresearch.cl/

A Closer Look

http://www.a-closer-look.com/

A Customer's Point of View

http://www.acpview.com/

Advanced Feedback

http://advancedfeedback.com

Agile Market Research

www.executivesolutionsmexico.com

Albatross CX

http://www.albatross-group.com

All Star Customer Service

http://www.mysteryshoppingexperts.com/

Alta 360 Research

https://www.alta360research.com/

A & A Merchandising

http://aamerch.com/

Amusement Advantage

https://www.amusementadvantage.com/shopent.asp

Ann Michaels & Associates, Ltd.

www.ishopforyou.com

Anonymous Insights, Inc.

https://a-insights.clientsmart.com/

Apartment Shoppe

https://www.apartmentmysteryshopper.com/

ARC Call Performance Solutions

www.arccps.com

ARC Consulting, LLC

http://www.arllc.com/

Ardent Services, Inc.

https://ardentservices.com/

Ath Power Consulting Corporation

https://www.athpower.com/

Athena Research Group, Inc.

www.athenaresearch.us

At Your Service Marketing

http://www.aysm.com/

Auditor Service

https://w3l.auditorservice.com/

Automotive Insights, LLC

http://www.automotiveinsights.com/

Baird Group

http://baird-group.com/

Bare International

https://www.bareinternational.com/

BDS Marketing

http://www.bdsmktg.com/

Bestmark

http://www.bestmark.com/become_a_shopper.htm

Big K Mystery Shopping

www.bigk.com.mx

Bild & Company

http://www.bildandco.com/

Blink Research

https://blinkresearch.com/

BMA Mystery Shopping

http://www.mystery-shopping.com

Business Evaluation Services

www.mysteryshopperservices.com

Business Observations

http://www.businessobservations.com

Business Solutions

http://bizshoptalk.com/

Campus Mystery Shopping

http://www.shopaudits.com/

Capstone Research

http://www.capstoneresearch.com/

Circle of Service

https://www.circle-of-service.com/

Cirrus Marketing Consultants

http://cirrusmktg.com/

Clarity CXM

https://claritycxm.com/

Clear Evaluations

www.clearevaluations.com

Client Smart

https://www.clientsmart.com/

Coast to Coast Scheduling Services, Inc.

https://www.ctcss.com/

comScore Mystery Shopper

https://ms.rentrak.com/

Confero Inc.

https://conferoinc.com/

Confidential Consumer

https://confidentialconsumer.com/

Confirm With Us, LLC

http://confirmwithus.com/

Constance Anderson & FCUD Associates/Member XP

https://www.memberxp.com/

Consumer Impressions

http://consumerimpressions.com/

Consumer Research Group

http://www.crg2000.com/

Consumer Service Analysis, Inc.

www.consumerserviceanalysis.com

Consumer@Site

www.consumeratsite.com

Count on Us

www.ucountonus.com

Coyle Hospitality

https://www.coylehospitality.com/

Creative Strategies

www.strategz.com

Cross Financial Group

https://www.crossfinancial.com/

Customer 1st

http://customer-1st.com

Customer Experience Experts

www.customer-experience-experts.com

Customer Impact

https://www.ci-gateway.com/shoppers/LoginShopper.norm.php

Customer Perspectives

www.customerperspectives.com

Customer Prophet

https://customerprophet.com

Customer Service Experts, Inc.

www.customerserviceexperts.com

Customer Service Perceptions

http://www.csperceptions.com/

Customer Service Profiles, LLC

http://csp.clientsmart.com

Data Quest Ltd.

https://www.sassieshop.com/sassie/SassieShopperSignup/Signup.php?EmsID=Sj7QE2rEx%2Bk%3D

David Sparks & Associates Research (DSA)

http://www.sparksresearch.com/

Daymon Interactions Consumer Experience Marketing

https://www.interactionsmarketing.com/

Devon Hill Associates (Medical)

https://devonhillassociates.com/

DSG Associates

https://www.dsgai.com/

Dynamic Advantage, Inc. (DA)

http://dynamic-advantage.com/about/professional-shoppers/

Electrum Branding

https://electrumbranding.com/

Elite CX Solutions

www.elitecxsolutions.com

Ellis Partners in Management Solutions (EPMS)

https://app.epmsonline.com/app/login?Destination=https://app.epmsonline.com/dispatch/shopper/interface/available

Evaluation Systems for Personnel (ESP)

http://espshop.com/

Faith Perceptions

https://faithperceptions.com/

Feedback Plus

http://www.feedbackplus.com/

Field Agent

https://www.fieldagent.net/

Fuzul

https://www.fuzul.com/

GAPbuster Worldwide (GBW)

http://www.gbw.solutions/

GFK Mystery Shops

https://www.gfkmysteryshops.com/index.norm.php

Global Compliance Services (GCS) Field Research

https://www.gcsresearch.com/Client/Login.aspx

Global Mystery Services

http://www.globalms.com.mx/

Grace Hill

http://www.thetrainingfactor.com

Greenhouse Marketing & Communications, Inc.

http://www.greenhousemarketing.ca/

Growth from Knowledge Mystery Shopping

https://www.gfk.com/

Grupo Avansa (Avansa Group)

http://grupoavansa.com/

Guest Check, Inc.

https://guestcheckinc.com/

Harland Clarke

https://www.harlandclarke.com/performance-analytics/prospect-experience-analytics/overview

Harris X

www.harrisx.com

Helion Research (Worldwide)

https://helionresearch.com/en/mystery_shoppers

Hendrickson Business Advisors, LLC

https://hendricksonbusinessadvisors.com/

High Standards

www.highstandardscolorado.com

Hope Research Group

www.hoperesearchgroup.com

Hospitality Consultants

http://www.hcreport.com

Hospitality Gem

www.hgem.com

Hospitality Now

http://hospitality-now.com/

HS Brands International

https://hsbrands.com/

ICC Decision Services

http://iccds.com/

ICU Associates, Inc.

http://www.icuassociates.com/home.html

Impact Marketing

www.impact-mrkt.com

IMYST

https://www.imyst.com/

Informa Research Services

https://financialintelligence.informa.com/contact/irs-mystery-shopper

Instant Replays (Audio & Video Performance Shopping)

https://instant-replays.clientsmart.com/

Instant Reply

http://www.mysteryshopservices.com/admin/shoppers/index.pl

Insula Research

www.insularesearch.com

Integrity Consultants, LLC

http://integrityconsultants.us/

Intelli Shop

www.intelli-shop.com

Intercept Insight, LLC

http://www.interceptinsight.com/

International Service Check

https://myaccount.internationalservicecheck.com/Default.aspx

Intouch Insight

https://www.intouchinsight.com/shop?gclid=CjwKCAjw-dXaBRAEEiwAbwCi5n3uu357L2j327gxz7HpV-2G-RPnGnFsdoKcPTtGSFY7gvDUi617thoCR0AQAvD_BwE

IPSOS Mystery Shopping

https://ipsosus.shopmetrics.com/document.asp?alias=loginMain

iSecretShop

https://isecretshop.com/

i-SPY Hospitality Audit Services

http://ispy4u.net/

Jancyn

http://www.jancyn.com/

JM Ridgway

https://jmridgway.com/

Jobslinger (Job Board)

http://www.jobslinger.com/

Kinesis Insight System

https://shopper.kinesis-cem.com/ShopperMenu.pl

KSS International

http://www.sassieshop.com/2kern/shoppers/LoginShopper.norm.php

Kupa'a Business Planner, Inc.

www.kupaabusinessplanners.com

Kush Research Group (Cannabis Industry)

http://www.kushcheck.com/

Live Shopper

https://liveshopper.com/

LP Innovations

http://www.lpinnovations.com/

LRA by Deloitte

https://www.sassieshop.com/sassie/SassieShopperSignu
p/Signup.php?EmsID=%252B5eZjftRu6k%253D

Management Consultant Group (MCG)

https://www.managementconsultantgroup.com/

Maritz Research

https://mysteryshopping.maritzcx.com/#/

Market Analytics International, Inc. (MMI)

http://marketanalytics.com/

Market Force Information, Inc.

https://www.marketforce.com/

Marketstat, Inc.

http://www.marketstat.com/

Market Viewpoint

http://www.marketviewpoint.com/

Marketwise Consulting Group, Inc.

http://www.marketwi.com/

Mars Research

https://marsresearch.com/

Measure Consumer Perspectives

https://measurecp.com/

Melinda Brody & Company

http://www.melindabrody.com/

Mercaplan

https://www.mercaplan.com/

Mercantile Systems

https://mercsystems.shopmetrics.com/document.asp?alias=login

Merchandise Concepts

https://merchandiseconcepts.com/

Michelson & Associates, Inc.

http://michelson.com/home.html

Mintel International Group Ltd.

https://shopper.mintel.com/user_login.php

Monterey Mystery Shopping

https://www.montereymysteryshopping.com/

MPACT

http://mpactgroupinc.com

MSP Services, LLC (Mystery Shopper Pros)

https://www.mysteryshopperpros.com/

mVentix, Inc.

https://www.mventix.com/

MysteryShopper.com

https://www.mystery-shopper.com/

Mystery Shoppers Inc.

http://www.mystery-shoppers.com/

Mystique Shopper

http://www.mystiqueshopper.com/

National Field-Link, Inc.

http://www.nf-link.com/

National Shopping Service Network

https://www.mysteryshopper.net/

New Image Marketing Research Corporation

https://shoppernewimagemarketing.archondev.com/m
Global/mLogin?OpenForm&origLoginReasonType=0
&desiredLoginURL=%2FNewImageMarketing%2Fsh
opperDefs.nsf

North Fork Research/Omnichannel Solutions, LLC

http://www.northforkresearch.com/

Norton|Norris Incorporated

https://nortonnorris.com/

N Site Market Research

http://www.nsiteinc.com/

NWLPC

https://nwlpc.com/

Opinions, Ltd.

http://www.opinionsltd.com/

Perception Strategies

http://www.perstrat.com/

Perfectly Frank, Inc.

http://perfectlyfrankinc.com/

PerformaLogics, Inc.

http://performalogics.com/

Person to Person Quality/Michael L. Mitchell

https://shopper.persontopersonquality.com/mGlobal/m Login?OpenForm&origLoginReasonType=0&desiredL oginURL=%2FPersontoPersonQuality%2FshopperDef s.nsf

Personnel Profiles, Inc.

http://ppiadvantage.com/

Pinnacle Financial Strategies

http://pinnaclemysteryshopping.com/

Preferred Investigation

www.preferredinvestigation.com

Premier Service, Inc.

https://premierservice.ca/

Presto Maps

www.prestomaps.com

Primo Solutions, LLC

http://www.primosolutionsllc.com/

Prism Intelligence

http://prismintelligence.com/mystery-shopping/

Promotion Network, Inc.

http://promotionnetworkinc.com/

QSI Specialists

http://www.qsispecialists.com/

Quality Assessments Mystery Shoppers

https://qams.shopmetrics.com/login.asp

Quality Assurance Consulting, Inc.

http://www.qacinc.com/

Quest for Best/Quest Associates, Inc.

http://questforbest.com/

Red Quanta

https://www.redquanta.com/

RD Associates Inc.

http://rdassociates.com/

Reality Based Group (RBG)

https://www.realitybasedgroup.com/shoppers-corner/shopper-login/

Reality Check

http://www.realitycheckservice.com/

Reflections Mystery Shopping

http://www.reflectionsms.com

Regal Hospitality Group

http://regalhg.com/

Remington Evaluations (Apartments)

http://remysteryshops.com/

Researchers Services Group

https://www.sassieshop.com/2rsg/shoppers/LoginShopper.norm.php

Restaurant Cops, LLC

http://www.restaurant-cops.com/

Rocky Mountain Merchandising & Research/Six Star Solutions

https://rockymm.com/

RQA, Inc.

https://www.rqa-inc.com/

Sales Quality Research Group

http://salesqualitygroup.com/

Satisfaction Services, Inc.

http://www.satisfactionservicesinc.com/

Second to None

https://shopperhub.second-to-none.com/index.html#/login

Secret Shopper

https://www.secretshopper.com/

See Level Human Experience

https://seelevelshoppers.com/

Sensors Quality Management Inc.

http://sqm.ca/index.php/en/

Sentry Marketing Group

http://www.sentrymarketing.com/

Service Alliance, Inc.

http://www.serviceallianceinc.com/

Service Check

http://servicecheck.com/

Service Connections, Inc.

http://www.serviceconnectionsinc.com/

Service Evaluation Concepts

https://serviceevaluation.com/

Service Evaluations

www.serviceevaluations.net

Service Impressions

http://www.serviceimpressions.com/

Service Performance Group, Inc.

https://spgweb.com/

Service Quality Development

http://sqd.lv/

Service Research Corporation

https://serviceresearch.com/

Service Scan

http://service-scan.com/

Service Scouts

http://servicescouts.com/

Service Sense

http://servicesense.com/

Service Sleuth/The Mershimer Group

http://www.mymysteryshop.com/shoppers/LoginShopper.norm.php

ServiceTrac (A Practice Max Company)

http://www.servicetrac.com/

Service with Style Hospitality Group

https://www.servicewithstyle.com/

Servimer

http://www.servimer.com

Shared Insight Inc.

https://www.sharedinsight.com/

Shop Metrics

https://www.shopmetrics.com/

Shop'n Chek Inc. (Mexico)

http://snc.com.mx/

Shoppers

https://www.sassieshop.com/2si/shoppers/LoginShoppe
r.norm.php

Shoppers Confidential Mystery Shopping Services

https://shoppersconfidential.com/

Shoppers Critique International (SCI)

https://shopperscritique.com/

Shoppers, Inc.

https://www.insightyoucanuse.com/

Shoppers View

https://shoppersview.com/

Shopping by Mystery

https://www.cpinsights.com/

Sinclair Customer Metrics

http://www.sinclaircustomermetrics.com/

SkilCheck Services, Inc.

http://skilcheck.com

Spies in Disguise

http://spiesindisguise.com/index/

Spot Check Services

http://www.spotcheckservices.com/

Stericycle Expert Solutions

http://www2.mysteryshops.com/

Strategic Reflections Inc.

https://stratreflections.shopmetrics.com/login.asp

Summit Scheduling & Editing

http://summitscheduling.com/

Sutter Marketing

https://www.sassieshop.com/2sutter/shoppers/LoginShopper.norm.php

Technology Store Shopper

http://te chnologystoreshopper.com/

Texas Shoppers Network, Inc.

http://texasshoppersnetwork.com/

The Brandt Group

https://thebrandtgroup.com/

The Consumer Insight

https://www.sassieshop.com/sassie/SassieShopperSignup/Signup.php?EmsID=FuAy69hzA1Q%3D

The Guest Check

http://www.theguestcheck.com/

The Performance Edge

http://pedge.com/

The Secret Shopper

https://thesecretshopper.archondev.com/mGlobal/mLogin?OpenForm&origLoginReasonType=0&desiredLoginURL=%2FTheSecretShopper%2FShopperDefs.nsf

The Service Quality Department

http://www.service-quality.com/

The Shadow Agency

https://www.theshadowagency.com/

The Source

https://thesourceagents.com/

Trend Source, Inc.

https://www.trendsource.com/

True BX

www.truebx.com

True Guest

http://trueguest.com

Verify International, Inc.

https://verifyinternational.com/shoppers/

Volition (Job Board)

http://jobs.volition.com/exec/sfs/jobboard

We Check (Formerly CRG Mystery Shopping)

http://www.sassieshop.com/2thecrg/shoppers/LoginShopper.norm.php

White Clay Shoppers

http://wcshoppers.com/

Winthrop Douglas

http://winthropdouglas.com/

Chapter 9

The Application Process

Filling out the application is the first step to becoming an independent contractor for mystery shopping companies. Each company has its own policies, procedures, and instructions to complete the application. It is imperative to answer all of the questions on the application and provide any attachments requested, such as, a writing sample, copy of your driver's license, a headshot, etc. The average for application completeness is between 75%-80%. That means that 20-25 out of every hundred applications are incomplete. If you submit an incomplete application don't expect to hear back from the mystery shopping company. They feel that if you can't be bothered to complete the application, then you are not likely to turn in complete reports with each shop.

When I started mystery shopping, I put in an application at every available mystery shopping company so I would have a wide variety of shops to choose from. I put all the basics of the application in a Word document and would copy and paste the information into each application. All of the applications ask for the same basic information, but some vary slightly. Some applications require a writing sample to ensure you have good grammar, spelling, punctuation, and that you can write a detailed, cohesive paragraph. I had my husband review my writing sample to make sure everything was copasetic before submitting it.

When you complete your writing sample, do so in Microsoft Word and then copy and paste the writing sample into the application. This will allow you to do a spelling and grammar check to ensure most things are corrected prior to submitting the writing sample. I also suggest having someone review your writing sample prior to submitting it. The spelling and grammar check doesn't catch everything so an extra set of eyes will ensure correctness.

The writing sample will have specific instructions regarding what you must write about. They may ask you to write an example of a time when you received excellent customer service or a time when you received poor customer service. They may ask you to write about what you think makes a great mystery shopper. You could also be required to describe an experience you had at an entertainment facility.

Here is a sample of a writing sample I submitted for an experience I recently had at an entertainment facility:

I recently went to the XXX Zoo with my entire family. When we arrived, we waited in line for 8 minutes and 23 seconds to buy the tickets. There were 12 people in line ahead of us. We went the weekend before school started back so it was a very busy day. When we purchased the entrance tickets to the zoo, we received a military discount. The cashier, Sam (5'8", female, long blond hair, early 20's) asked if we wanted to purchase Sky Ride tickets and we purchased those as well. Sam offered the upsell in addition to the military discount per zoo policy. Sam gave us a coin for each entrant and explained the coin would be used to choose which animal project we wanted to support. Sam explained that the program is called Quarters for Conservation which allows the zoo entrants to vote for their favorite conservation project. Sam further explained that the conservation project that received the most support would receive the most funding on a proportional basis.

We then entered the zoo and we each voted for the conservation project we wanted to support. We then proceeded down the path towards the Yellow Zone towards the giraffes. We went to the Giraffe Feeding Experience hut and purchased 5 sets of lettuce to feed the giraffes. The four boys and I feed the giraffes. We then went on to Encounter Africa and the Elephant Barn. We took approximately 40 pictures through the Yellow Zone.

Another important thing to do when completing the application is to ensure that you have proper sentence structure and punctuation. Make sure each sentence begins with a capital letter and that you do not use abbreviations. If you have trouble with grammar, sentence structure, spelling, punctuation, or poor writing skills, I would suggest taking the writing course offered by the MSPA. This training covers the writing skills needed when completing mystery shop reports.

The vast majority of mystery shopping companies allow you to sign up for shop notification emails. I suggest having an email address just for mystery shopping because depending on the number of companies you sign up for it can be an overwhelming amount of emails. As you can see there are over 250 companies listed in the previous chapter which can generate a considerable amount of emails. This allows you to see shops as soon as they become available and apply for them quickly.

When completing mystery shop applications, you will be required to either provide your social security number (SSN) or an employer identification number (EIN) to work for a mystery shopping company. An EIN is a number that can be obtained from the IRS that you can use to conduct business. An EIN is easy to apply for and prevents others from seeing your SSN. Please check the IRS website for the qualifications you must meet to apply for an EIN.

You will also be required to fill out a demographic section on the application. This is not something you see on a normal employment application. Mystery shopping companies can and do discriminate based on demographics. In a normal employment situation this would be illegal but in this instance it is legal. Clients hire mystery shopping companies to find mystery shoppers who fit the demographics of their average customer. A company that has a client base of mostly teenagers would request teenagers to conduct the shop as it would match the demographic they usually serve.

Independent contractors are treated differently than employees by the law. This discrimination provides accurate market research for companies and allows the client to provide better customer service moving forward. Another example of this would be a barber shop whose clientele is all male or a strip club. Both businesses would likely request male shoppers to conduct these shops because this matches the demographic of their average patron.

Alcohol and tobacco checks generally have age restrictions. If a liquor store wants to ensure its employees are properly carding customers, they will generally have shoppers between the ages of 21-25 shop the location to ensure compliance. These types of shops are essential to liquor stores because they can lose their liquor license or pay a huge fine if they sell to someone under age. It would make no sense to assign this type of shop to someone who is 70 years old. The employee could tell by looking at the customer that they are of age. This would not help the store to ensure they are being compliant overall.

This type of discrimination is legal because it is a requirement to successfully complete the shop. For example, I have attended many Medicare seminars as mystery shops to sign up for a Part C Medicare plan. The requirement to complete these shops is that you must be at least 45 years of age or older. In this scenario, you are either looking for a Medicare Part C plan for yourself or a parent. It would not be logical for a 21-year-old to attend a Medicare seminar because someone that age would not have the need.

The demographic section also asks what kind of cars you own or have access to use. A company may need someone with a Ford vehicle to conduct a service shop at a Ford dealership. The demographic section also asks if you have children and what their ages are. There are some shops that require children to be present to complete the shop. A company could be checking to make sure that their employees are not selling "R" rated video games to children under the age of 18.

A mystery shopping company may be looking for a person of a certain race to ensure people are not being discriminated against. For example, a watchdog organization may have gotten word that a housing community is discriminating against African Americans. The watchdog organization would possibly hire an African American shopper and a Caucasian shopper to go in on the same day and ask the same questions. This would verify the differences each shopper experienced when attempting to rent a house or apartment.

I have seen this happen on a documentary. A watchdog organization sent in an African American applicant to apply to rent an apartment. The African American applicant was told that there were no apartments for rent at this time. The Caucasian applicant then went in to apply to rent an apartment. The Caucasian applicant was told that there was an apartment available for rent and was given an application to fill out. Each applicant had a hidden video camera to capture the discrimination. These videos gave the watchdog organization the proof they needed to prove discrimination is occurring.

Another item that is required in the demographics section is your annual income. The income you post on your mystery shopping application is something that helps identify your current lifestyle. The things you have experienced in life can vary greatly based on your income. A person who makes $150,000 a year leads a very different lifestyle than someone who makes $20,000 a year. A shopper who has a higher income normally buys high end items and goes out to fine dining establishments on a regular basis. If you make $20,000 a year, you are not very likely to go out and spend $500 on a dinner for two or purchase a Rolex watch. The individual with the higher income would be a better judge of quality at a fine dining establishment because they frequent such locations.

It is important to answer all demographic questions with as much detail as possible. When you complete the demographics' section with as much detail as possible you allow the mystery shopping company to offer you more shops. Mystery shopping companies will do a search of their databases to find shoppers who meet certain qualifications and offer those people the shop they are looking to fill.

IC Pro (Independent Contractor Professional) is a mystery shopper registry. This registry has been endorsed by more than 50 mystery shopping companies. Some mystery shopping companies will give priority to a mystery shopper who is registered with IC Pro. When you register for Independent Contractor Pro status you receive more shops. Shops are given to mystery shoppers based on your IC Pro rating. The higher your IC Pro rating the more shops you are likely to get.

When you are signed up with IC Pro, your account is connected to all of your SASSIE accounts. You must also have a Jobslinger account and connect it with your IC Pro account. Each SASSIE account you have will show your IC Pro badge. You go to http://www.jobslinger.com/ICPro to fill out the information on the form. You don't have to fill out all of the information but the more information you fill out, the higher your rating. You must fill in the W-9 information to get an IC Pro score. A W-9 is required for all mystery shopping companies. A W-9 is a form required by the IRS.

When a business pays an independent contractor $600 or more over the course of a tax year, it is required to report these payments to the IRS on an information return called form 1099-MISC. Businesses use the name, address and Social Security or tax identification number from form W-9 to complete form 1099-MISC. The Form W-9 is used to file information with the IRS. The W-9 does not expire but the business you are working with can request an updated W-9 to maintain accurate records of their independent contractors.

Chapter 10

Getting Assignments

Once you have completed your application and have been accepted by the mystery shopping company it is time to apply for and conduct shops. Most mystery shopping companies have restrictions on the number of shops you can accept when you first start. As you gain experience and complete more shops the number of shops you are allowed to take at one time increases. This is done because the mystery shopping companies want to make sure you are reliable before they allow you to start taking on more shops.

You have discretion about the types of shops you take and the distance you travel to conduct those shops. There are some shops that are hard to fill for many reasons. This can be because they do not have mystery shoppers in the area, the mystery shopping company is approaching a deadline, or they are not popular shops. I have taken shops in rural areas because they could not find anyone to complete them. The more flexible you are, the more money you can make. I made $425 one weekend because I was willing to travel a considerable distance and complete five shops along the way. Bonuses are often given for hard to fill shops.

When a scheduler knows you are flexible and willing to take last minute shops, they will generally reach out to those shoppers first by email to see if you would like the shop before they send out a mass email to ask for volunteers. The more reliable you are, the more likely you are to be offered these special shops with increased pay. I always try to develop a good relationship with the schedulers because they can help you get the best paying and "special" shops you are looking for. The best way I found to create these relationships is by being reliable and turning in high quality reports. Schedulers always look to the people that are most dependable because they know they don't have to worry about the shopper "flaking" and then later having to reassign the shop to someone else.

When you see a shop offered on a mystery shopping site it will normally have some restrictions. These restrictions include things like you cannot have shopped this location in the last 30 days, that the shop must be completed between the 1st-25th of the month, and the shop cannot be conducted on Thursdays or holidays. These are some examples of the restrictions that could be listed on a shop and these vary widely by shop. You must choose a date to conduct the shop that conforms to these restrictions.

There are certain shops that pay more based on special requirements for the shop. For example, if you have a Military ID or access behind airport security you will likely be paid more to complete shops that have these requirements. It can be difficult for mystery shopping companies to find shoppers who have Military ID's or access behind security at an airport. Therefore these shops have higher fees.

Schedulers have a very difficult job especially when they schedule a shopper to complete a shop and then they "flake". This happens an astonishing 25% of the time. When this occurs, the scheduler has to find another shopper to complete the shop. There are many things a scheduler looks at before they schedule a shop to someone. They look at the requirements given to them by the client. The shop could require someone with a specific age, race, gender, or income level. The scheduler must make sure they have someone who meets the guidelines given to them by the client. They will cross-reference the requirements from the client with the shoppers that have applied to conduct the shop and assign it to the shopper that is most appropriate to conduct the shop.

If everyone that applies meets the requirements given by the client, then the scheduler has the discretion to give the assignment to any shopper. The scheduler will look at the demographics of each shopper, writing samples, and previous shop scores before making their decision. A scheduler wants to ensure you are reliable and will properly complete the report required for the shop. You are more likely to get assigned a shop when you complete all assignments that you have accepted in a timely manner; you completely high-quality reports with proper spelling, grammar, punctuation, and excellent writing skills; and above all you are a professional.

When requesting a shop, you must follow the guidelines and choose a date within the guidelines provided. Some shops will require you to complete the shop within a date range and some will require you to pick a specific date within a date range that adheres to the guidelines. That is why I cannot emphasize enough the importance of reading the guidelines prior to requesting or accepting a shop. The date that you plan to conduct the shop is very important. When you state a specific date that you will conduct the shop, this is the date the scheduler is expecting you to complete the shop. The scheduler may be required by the client to have someone shop the location every three days. That is why it is essential to give the date you will complete the shop and complete it on the day specified. If you submit a request to do the shop on Thursday and something has come up, you can email the scheduler that you are assigned the shop on Thursday and would like to switch it to Friday. When you have an open line of communication with the scheduler and are specific about the change you are more likely to be accommodated. A scheduler would much rather change the date you are conducting the shop then trying to find someone else to complete it. It is important to not make this a habit but there can be flexibility with completing shops.

When a scheduler is choosing someone to complete the shop and the date range is from the 1st-25th. The shopper that requests the earliest date is the one that is more likely to get it. If you have two shoppers that put in for the same shop and Shopper A stated they would complete the shop on the 1st and Shopper B stated they would complete the shop on the 25th, Shopper A is more likely to be assigned the shop. This is because if the shopper doesn't complete the shop on the 1st then the scheduler can easily reschedule the shop with another shopper to complete before the deadline.

When applying for a shop you may be required to take a test or meet certain qualifications prior to being awarded a shop. There are certain shops where you must know the features of the product prior to completing a shop. Sometimes the test includes the instructions to a shop, and you must answer questions regarding the requirements of the shop. I have taken some tests that are rather complicated and others that are very simple.

Most fees for shops are set but some can be negotiated. When a scheduler cannot find someone to complete a shop, they will likely provide a bonus to get the shop completed. When there are shops that are hard to fill you can sometimes negotiate the fee you receive. If there is a location that is 30 miles from your house and the shop fee is $6 but the shop cannot be filled, you can in most cases request a higher fee. There are some locations where shoppers do not live or are not willing to go. When you come across these shops you can likely negotiate. I have been called at home to do a shop that was 30 miles from my house and was able to negotiate a fee that was double the normal fee because the mystery shopping company could not find anyone to fill the shop.

In this instance if you see a shop not being filled that is coming close to the deadline to complete, you can send an email to the scheduler and offer to do the shop. I would send an email that says: I have noticed that you have a shop available in Anywhere, CO that is due tomorrow and you have been unavailable to fill this shop. I am willing to conduct this shop if you still need someone, I am 30 miles from the location and could conduct the shop for an increased fee of $10. The scheduler may reply back that they can pay you the increased fee or may simply say they do not have money available for a bonus for this shop. This shows that you are willing to help out whenever possible and puts you on the scheduler's list of people they can count on with short notice. If you do, then complete the shop without the bonus this could definitely put you in line for top shops.

Chapter 11

How to do a Mystery Shop

When conducting a mystery shop, the company will advise you if there are any risks associated with completing the shop. These risks include things like negatively affecting your credit score because your credit report must be run. When you begin work with a mystery shopping company, you sign a contract with them that tells you the method of payment, the average length of time before payments are received, the required guidelines for each shop, and the no show policy for not completing a shop.

Before you leave to conduct a shop, it is imperative that you read the required report prior to conducting the shop. This is essential because the report has a series of questions that must be answered during the shop. You should know what questions you need to answer prior to completing the shop and the requirements that are required. When you miss a requirement, your shop would not be accepted the mystery shopping company and you would not receive payment. Employees are advised not to "mystery shop spot" because that can annoy customers. When employees "mystery shop spot" they try to figure out who the mystery shopper is and make sure all standards are met for that customer. This can lead to annoyance by the customer because they feel they are being bothered.

When conducting a shop, it is essential that all of the directions are followed. When you do a gas shop at a convenience store, for example, it may state to purchase gas at the pump with a credit card and make a purchase inside with cash. It is essential that all instructions are followed, or your shop will be rejected and you will not be paid.

Some mystery shops have a considerable amount of questions. During some shops, I will put a copy of the questions in my purse and go into the bathroom to look at them to make sure I have not overlooked anything during the shop. Almost all shops require you to check the bathroom and report on cleanliness and supplies available. When I do that I go into the stall and give a quick glance of the questions to ensure I am meeting all requirements. I cannot stress enough how important it is to not only read the shop you are going to conduct but also the Independent Contractor Agreement (ICA) you sign when starting with the mystery shopping company because it can have various restrictions including a restriction to not use a voice recorder on shops and other various restrictions.

When conducting mystery shops, it is essential to schedule enough time to conduct the shop, complete the report, and enter it into the system. Make sure you confirm the shop right away and print it out. I always print out a copy of the shop and instructions to review prior to the conducting the shop. That way I know what is required on the shop. When I print the shops out, I put them in date order so I stay organized. I double check to make sure there is not part of the shop due prior to the shop due date. Some shops are two-part shops where a phone call is required prior to going to the location.

When conducting mystery shops, it is essential to schedule enough time to conduct the shop, complete the report, and input it into the system. Make sure you confirm the shop right away when you are assigned the shop. I also suggest printing the shop and instructions right away too. I print each shop completely and put them in date order. I read each shop prior to ensure that no portion of the shop needs to be completed prior to the due date. An example would be if I needed to go into a location to make a purchase but needed to call the location the day prior to the purchase. This would be a two-part shop and I would need to ensure I made the call the day prior to making the purchase to correctly complete the shop and get paid. When I made the call, I would make sure I filled out the call section of the shop right away, so I did not forget any information from that call.

There are some mystery shoppers that prefer to use digital voice recorders when conducting mystery shops, so they have the entire interaction recorded. This can be helpful to get exact quotes from employees. I choose not to use a digital voice recorder when conducting shops unless it is a requirement. The digital voice recorder that I do use has a microphone on the top of the recorder. This allows me to put the recorder in my bra and not obstruct the microphone. I get amazing audio from this recorder. Here is a picture of the digital voice recorder that I use.

When conducting a shop that requires a voice recording you must upload the voice recording in addition to the written report. In some rare instances you will only be required to upload the voice recording. A digital voice recorder works best with an external microphone unless you have one like I do that prevents distortion and has a microphone on the top that will not be obstructed. I highly suggest practicing using the voice recorder at home where you can test to ensure you have the recorder set at the right volume. You should also look in the mirror to ensure that the red light that shows you are recording is not visible. I practiced recording conversations prior to doing on a mystery shop to ensure that all the settings were correct, that the I was able to hear and understand the recording, and to make sure that I did not need to make any adjustments. I also made sure that I had enough battery life before I went on the shop to ensure that the voice recorder would work.

I turn on the recorder when I am in my car so that the employees of the location do not know they are being recorded. You can say in your car what time it is before you enter the location, so the recording has the time recorded. You can then use the time lapse feature on the voice recorder for timings. Make sure that you do not turn off the voice recorder until you are in your car so that you are not seen.

I live in Colorado which is a one-party consent state which means that you only need one party who is involved in the conversation to consent to a voice recording. The laws vary by state and country.

You can mystery shop no matter where you are. I always mystery shop on vacations. This may sound counter-productive and may seem like you may not be able to enjoy your vacation if you mystery shop on it but actually the opposite is true. Mystery shopping during your vacation allows you to do more with a smaller budget. I choose a lot of my vacations based on mystery shops that are available. If I want to travel to a certain state, I will find a hotel mystery shop in that state. I will also look for airline shops, tourist attraction shops, spa shops, and dining shops where I am staying. When all items are not on one shop then I have to fill out multiple shop reports, but I feel it is worth it to get a free vacation. You do have to do lots of planning and keep your eye out for these shops. I do this by checking available shops and planning accordingly.

You can find shops for airline tickets when a company would like the service received on the flight and at their airport lounge club reviewed. These shops are fun because you get a free flight and get to spend time in the airline lounge club. Hotel shops usually includes the cost of the hotel for the number of nights of the stay, tip for the bellhop (arrival &

departure), tip for valet (arrival & departure), tip for housekeeping,

You can sometimes find a shop, such as, a casino shop that has many components to it and you only need to fill out one shop report.

You should complete every shop that you accept. There are extreme circumstances when it is okay to cancel a shop, but you should do this sparingly. When there is bad weather the mystery shopping company will likely send out an email to advise you of an extended period to complete the shops in your area. Four years ago, we had a major snowstorm in Colorado and the mystery shopping companies sent out emails to advise shoppers in the area they had an extra two days to complete their shops. They advised shoppers that if you had a shop scheduled you could conduct the shop up to two days after it was scheduled without penalty. The mystery shopping companies understand when there is bad weather and are not looking to have anyone get hurt and will adjust. When you have an emergency, it is acceptable to cancel a shop but this should be a rare occurrence. There have been some shoppers who have cancelled shops six different times because their grandmother died. The average person has two grandmothers. While schedulers are sympathetic to emergencies you should know that they have many experiences like this and are sometimes cynical. That is why I say cancel a shop on a very rare occurrence.

You can never ask another shopper to complete a shop for you. If you have someone in mind that could complete the shop in your place you need to check with the scheduler. Some shops have certain requirements that must be met in order to be accepted by the client. If the shopper assigned to the shop does not meet the requirements it will not be accepted by the client. This means the person you asked to complete the shop will not be paid and you will receive a 0 score for not completing the shop. My husband had a shop at a local restaurant, and something came up so I completed it. We simply sent a message to the scheduler and asked if it would be okay. The scheduler approved the change and assigned me to the shop.

The first thing you should do when you are assigned a shop is to print the shop and read it through. You must make sure that you go to the correct location on the day and time frame assigned. If you are assigned to complete a shop on Monday at the north location between the hours of 5 p.m. and 7 p.m. you must follow those specific instructions. If you shop outside those hours or are at the wrong location your shop will not be accepted and you will not be paid. This happens more often than you think. It is frustrating not only for the shopper but also the scheduler because the shop must be rescheduled because it was an invalid shop.

The instructions for the shop can sometime be difficult to understand or contradict themselves. When you first print out the shop make sure you fully understand what is required and if there are any contradictions send an email to the scheduler to get clarification. This has happened to me on multiple occasions. Most recently I was doing a dinner shop which stated that I must order an appetizer, entrée, and dessert for the shop to be accepted. Then later in the shop instructions it stated that if an appetizer was ordered the shop would not be valid. The shop instructions contradicted each other. I sent an email to the scheduler to inquire as to whether an appetizer should be ordered based on this contradiction. The scheduler emailed me back that an appetizer should be ordered, and the shop instructions were wrong. The scheduler sent me an email back and thanked me for pointing out the contradiction and advised me that the shop instructions would be updated going forward so other shoppers would not be confused.

The shop you are assigned to will generally have a scenario attached to the shop. For example, if you are assigned a cell phone shop it will have a scenario that must be followed once you arrive at the location. The scenario could be that you currently own the XYZ cell phone and are looking to upgrade to a new smartphone and would like some recommendations from the salesperson. The shop could require you to get 3 recommendations and to inquire about a specific cell phone if not mentioned as one of the recommendations. Much of the time these cell phone shops require you to get the business card of the salesperson that assisted you, their description, or even possibly a picture of the location.

There are some shops where you do not make a purchase and you must raise an objection. This could be an objection given to you specifically in the scenario to see how the employee responds to that objection. For a cell phone shop, you could be required to object regarding the price of the cell phone being too expensive. This gives the employee the opportunity to offer that affordable payment plan provided by the company. These objections are important because the client wants to see if the salesperson is following company procedure and recommending the payment plan.

You may not be required to raise an objection for a shop but may want to have one ready if you are not making a purchase. When I conduct cell phone shops, for example, a purchase is not required, and the salesperson will normally ask you to sign up for the service or purchase a phone. In this instance, I advise the salesperson that I need to speak with my husband before making a final

decision which gives me any easy out. My husband says
the same thing.

Chapter 12

Writing the Report

On most mystery shop reports that you complete you will need to upload item(s) to the report. These item(s) include receipts from the location, pictures, a pamphlet or brochure, a business card, or other identified items. Each report you are given to complete prior to the mystery shop has specific instructions that must be followed for your report to be accepted and for you to be paid. It is essential that you review the report immediately upon acceptance of the report. There are some requirements that require you to call before you go to the location. The report will also tell you the dates and time you can complete the shop. There may also be timings that you need to get and enter into the report. This can be done multiple ways. There is a stopwatch feature on most smart phones that will show you the amount of time that has past. I use a Vivo Fit because this is something that a vast majority of the population has, and people pay little attention to it. I start the timer before entering the facility and the casually look at my Vivo Fit to begin timing and note the end time on my Vivo Fit. I then text myself the amount of time the requirement took. People text all the time so this does not make you look obvious.

An example of a narrative at a casual restaurant:

I entered Bob's Burger Bar at 5:02 p.m. There were six customers in line waiting to order. I waited in line for 8 minutes before I reached the cashier. The cashier was named Joe (male, 5' 10", short brown hair, early 30s, moustache). He greeted me immediately upon reaching the cash register at 5:12 p.m. Joe advised me that the daily special was the double bacon burger with Bob's mystery sauce and asked if I would like to order the special. I told Joe that I would like to order the special. Joe asked if I would like onion rings, curly fries, or waffle fries with the special. I ordered the waffle fries. Joe asked what size drink I would like with my meal. I ordered a large drink. I was given my receipt without asking for it. Joe advised me that my number would be called, and I could pick up my meal and the counter at the end. I went over to the soda machine to fill my cup. The area that had the soda machine was clean with no trash on the counter. The ice machine was full. The condiment area which was next to the soda machine was clean and organized. All of the condiment containers were full. I sat down at the table and watched the employees as I waited for my meal. The restaurant floor was immaculate, and the employees cleaned off the empty tables within 30 seconds of customers leaving. My number was called to pick up my meal 6 minutes and 32 seconds after I placed my order. The employee at the pick-up counter (Sue; female, early 20s, long blond hair up in a bun, 5'8") went over my order to ensure I received exactly what I ordered. My order was correct and prepared exactly as ordered. My double bacon burger with Bob's mystery sauce was cooked well as ordered. The burger was juicy and was well seasoned. My waffle fries were hot, crispy, and well-seasoned. On the way out, the cashier (Joe) told me to have a fantastic night and to come again soon.

The shop report form you fill out has a series of questions that must be answered and observations that you need to make during the shop. The observations include things like the outside of the building being clean and well maintained, the bathrooms being cleaned and fully stocked, how long it takes from the time you ordered your food until it arrives, if the condiment bare is clean and organized, if the ice machine is full, the name of the cashier that took your order, a description of that person, etc. A shop form can contain numerous questions and observations that are required on a shop. There are many ways shoppers ensure that they answer all of the required questions and make all the necessary observations on their shop form. Some shoppers make notes on their cell phone and text themselves the notes. This makes it look like you are receiving a text message from someone and are simply returning the text. The person at the location has no idea that you are texting yourself. Some shoppers will call themselves and leave a message on their cell phone where they tell themselves the observations they need to make and listen to it during the shop. When a shopper does this it just looks as if someone called them and they are listening to the message that was left for them. I put a copy of the shop report in my purse and go into the bathroom and look at it to make sure I answer all the required questions and make all the required observations. There is an app you can use called "Shop It Stealth Notes" that allows for notes, recordings, photos, time lapse recording, location verification, and many other features. I have read some reviews on the app but have never used the app myself. The way you take notes is a personal preference. I would try a few different ways and see which way works best for you.

On most mystery shop forms there is a section for comments about good or bad service. These comments are not subjective. They are objective. Subjective information is based on personal opinions, interpretations, emotions, and judgment. Objective information is fact-based, measurable, and observable. A subjective comment about waiting in line at the grocery store would be I experienced horrible customer service at the grocery store because I had to wait in line forever. An objective statement about waiting in line at the grocery store would be I stood in line at the grocery store for 23 minutes until I reached the cashier. There were 8 customers in line in front of me. When the 10th customer entered the line a 2nd register was not opened as per company policy. In both examples you are explaining a bad customer service experience, but the key is to do it objectively with facts, measurements, and observations. Mystery shopping companies are looking for objective statements.

Some assignments require you to get the names of employees that you interact with during your shop. This is easy if they are wearing a name tag, their name is embroidered on their shirt, or they have a name plate at their desk. The cashier's names are also sometimes listed on the receipt. When all else fails ask. There are several ways to get someone's name without being obvious. You can say any of the following:

1) You look familiar. What is your name?

2) You have been very helpful. What is your name?

3) Could I get your name because if I have additional questions, I would like to ask for you?

4) Sorry I forgot your name.

5) You can call the store and ask the name of the person helping you because you would like to know their name if you have any further questions.

When noting someone's name on a shop report make sure you also put a description of them. There have been instances where employees have changed name tags so an employee cannot be properly identified. I was doing a shop and one employee had everyone's name tag on. This actually made it really easy for me to find out her name because I simply said wow you have so many names, which one is yours. It made her laugh and she told me her name. I always put the description because you just never know. (Gender, Age, Height, Hair Color & Length). For example (Female, early 20's, 5'8", Long Red Hair)

There are several timings that you could be required to get during a shop. These include but are not limited to:

- Time you arrived

- Time you departed

- How long you were at the location

- How long after you entered the location were you greeted

- How long did you wait in line

- How long was the checkout process

- How long between the time you ordered your food and when you received it

These required timings vary by shop, but these are some examples. I use my VivoFit to do my timings. Most of the population wears some kind of activity tracker and looking at your tracker doesn't arouse suspicion. I naturally look at mine several times a day even when I am not conducting a shop to see how many steps, I have taken so far that day. When you do things that are natural people don't really pay attention to you.

The "Shop It Lite" app allows you to take notes and it looks like you are texting. The app also provides a time stamp when you press a button on the app. There is also a panic button on the app which pops up a crossword puzzle when pushed. This feature can be used if you think an employee has seen you entering information.

Before you submit your report make sure the timings are correct and make sense. For example, if you were at the grocery store for 24 minutes and spent 19 minutes waiting in line and 8 minutes shopping for the item you bought this would not be possible. Based on your timings you reported you would have been in the grocery store for 27 but based on the narrative you wrote you were only in the grocery store for 24 minutes. When the editor looks at your report, they would see that your report contradicts itself and would send it back to you. You will be required to make corrections to the report before it can be submitted to the client. This will lower your report score and overall inconvenience the editor. Make sure to double check everything on your report prior to submitting it.

Photos are sometimes a requirement for a shop. The photos that are required vary by shop. Make sure you read the instructions thoroughly to ensure you understand the photos required for the shop. When a photo is not taken by the guidelines your shop will be rejected. If the requirements state that you must take a picture of your meal with no bites taken you must take the photo exactly as stated in the instructions. There are some instructions that require you to take a picture within 2 minutes of receiving your meal. The photos that you take are time stamped so they know exactly what time you took the photo. The company wants a photo immediately to see if it is steaming and what it looks like right away as you received it. If you receive your food and do not meet the requirement the company can see this on their video footage. It is important to follow the instructions specifically so your shop will be accepted.

Today with the mass use of social media it is common to see people taking pictures of their food and posting it to social media. You can look at some people's social media accounts and see pictures from everything they did that day including everything they ate. If you take a picture of your meal nobody will think twice about it. They will just think you are posting the picture to your Instagram account. You don't need to worry about looking out of place taking pictures because people do it now all day long.

When not specified I use my cash back or miles rewards card, so I get an added bonus to completing the shop.

Most shops require a receipt. The receipt is usually either scanned and uploaded or taken as a digital photo and uploaded. There are some rare cases where you need to mail in the receipt. I have done some movie shops where I have had to mail in receipts.

Make sure you read the instructions to see what you need to do if you are not offered a receipt. I always put the receipt in my wallet to make sure I have it when I get home and I don't lose it. I then go home and scan and upload the receipt. I then tape the receipt to a piece of paper, write the date, location I went to, the amount of the receipt, and I put it in my 3-ring binder. I write the information on the paper because sometimes receipts fade over time and that way you will not lose the information. You will need that at the end of the year to complete your taxes.

When you make a purchase and return, I suggest that you make a copy of the first receipt in case you are not given the original back. If you make a copy and the original is not given back, you will be covered because you will have a copy.

If you get a receipt that is not legible send an email immediately to the mystery shopping company to find out what they would like you to do. You can sometimes make a copy of the receipt and darken it up so it can be read. If you do not get a receipt it is important to contact the scheduler immediately to determine what they would like you to do. In some instances, they can work around this but there are instances where it will invalidate the shop.

There are times when things can go wrong during a shop. Here are a few things that could possibly go wrong during a shop:

- You go to the wrong location

- You don't follow the scenario
- You didn't get a business card or the required item
- Something happened to make them remember you
- Your report was rejected

There are certain times when the something goes wrong, and it can be fixed. There are some instances when something goes wrong, and you can't fix it. This is why I have said so many times to make sure you carefully read the instructions to make sure you make no mistakes. I did once forget a business card for a shop. I was able to go back because it was a big store and grab a business card without anyone paying attention to me. It just depends on the circumstances. If you have any doubts you can email the scheduler with anything that went wrong, and they can assist you in figuring out what to do. It is better however if you do not have anything go wrong because it makes everything much easier.

When you have completed your shop, the next step is to complete the report. When you first start the reports can take a while because you are not used to filling them out. You will get quicker at filing them out with practice. The amount of time it takes to fill out the report varies greatly with the information required. If the report is a simple checkbox form, then it may only take a few minutes to fill it out. If the report requires extensive narratives, then it could take hours. The more reports you complete the better you will get at the process.

Narratives can be difficult to write if you are not used to writing them. The narratives that you supply in your report should be objective and not subjective. Subjective information is based on personal opinions, interpretations, emotions, and judgment. Objective information is fact-based, measurable, and observable. A subjective comment about waiting in line at the grocery store would be I experienced horrible customer service at the grocery store because I waited in line forever. An objective statement about waiting in line at the grocery store would be I stood in line at the grocery store for 23 minutes. There were 8 customers in line in front of me. When the 10th customer entered the line a second register was not opened per company policy.

When you get ready to complete your report make sure you have all your information gathered. You will need your receipts, photos, forms, notes, timings, and any other documents required. Most reports are completed online. I always print out the form prior to completing the shop. I answer all the questions on the printed-out form and then enter it into the form on the website. Most reports are due within 24 hours of completing the shop, but some are due sooner.

There are a variety of different questions that mystery shop reports can have. There are simple yes/no questions were you simply answer yes, no, or N/A. You answer N/A if the question is not applicable to your situation. There are some questions that require simple answers like how long you were on hold when you called a location. When you receive a question like this, and it does not apply you simply put N/A.

There are questions that require narratives. Comments are always required for any "no" answer. You must explain why the standard was not met. When the report requires all narratives, you must describe exactly what happened from beginning to end with an objective description. The reports you turn in are graded. Most mystery shopping companies grade your report on a scale from 1-10. There are some companies that grade on a percentage from 1%-100%. There are a few other variations, but most companies grade from a 1-10. The ranking of your report is very important because you can sign up for future shops based on the ranking you receive on the report.

Timings asked for on the report may be an exact time of the day (i.e., 5:32 p.m.) or the amount of time it took for something to happen (i.e., like waiting in line for 1 minute and 23 seconds)

Make sure your report is complete and correct before submission. It is important to save your answers when entering your report every 15 minutes to prevent losing your work. I learned the hard way. I had typed a report with a considerable amount of narratives, and something happened to my internet connection and I lost everything that I had entered. I now type all of my narratives in a Word document and cut and paste them into the report to make sure I have the information typed in because I lose it at any point. I also save my reports now every 15 minutes, as well.

When typing narratives make sure you look for the minimum number of characters required for the narrative and any maximums listed. When completing a narrative if you do not enter enough characters or too many your narrative will not be accepted. Make sure you look to see what the requirements are and make sure you meet them. I have all my hand-written reports that I have filled out for mystery shopping in a bank box. I keep them for a period of three years in case I ever get audited, so I have proof of each shop I conducted along with the receipts and mileage records. After the three-year period I shred the documents. In the United States, the IRS will audit up to three years back so that is why I keep three years' worth of records.

With you are uploading your report, you must also upload receipts, documents, business cards, etc. Instructions may say to upload the documents as a JPEG file which is a picture or it may require you to upload a PDF file which you can create by scanning the image.

Make sure you read the instructions because some will want you to write the shop number on the business card or other information. You must make sure the shop is done correctly. You should ensure the following:

- Right day
- Right time of day
- Right location
- Proper documentation
- All questions answered
- All guidelines followed
- Met minimum time requirements at the location
- Made purchase (if required)

- Returned purchase (if required)

- Ask all questions required

- Followed scenario

- Comments for all "no" answers on questions

- Proper spelling, grammar, punctuation, and complete sentences

- Well-written narratives

- No opinions unless asked for

Reports are rated based on these criteria. The better report you submit, the better your score. Most companies require a high report average to accept most shops. The majority of mystery shopping companies rate your mystery shopping reports on a scale from 1-10. Most companies that have this scale require an average report score of 8 or better to accept or be given shops.

There are some questions in reports that do require an opinion. Read these questions carefully and answer the questions exactly as asked. For example, two questions could be similar but are not the same. Here are two questions that are asked on shops reports that are similar but require very different answers.

1) If you were looking for a new salon would you choose this salon?

2) Would you return to this salon and spend your own money?

You may be someone who doesn't ever go to salons unless someone else pays for it. Remember when answering the question, you are playing the part of someone who would go to a salon on a normal basis.

Most shop reports require comments. When asked a question that has a no answer you must provide a comment as to why the location did not meet the standard. An example question would be: Were all the lights working properly in the parking lot? If the answer is no, you need to put a comment to explain why that standard was not met. For example: No. There was one light out in the parking lot.

When writing narratives, it is important to use adjectives. You should quote the employee whenever possible. Never compare locations or competitors. This is not what the mystery shopping company is looking for. They are looking to see if this location has met the standards.

Chapter 13

Getting Paid

The amount of money you can make from mystery shopping varies greatly depending upon the type of shops you take. There are three types of mystery shops with regards to how a mystery shopping company pays you for a shop. There are reimbursement only shops, set fee shops, and combined shops (this includes a set fee and a reimbursement). The first shop is a reimbursement only shop. Reimbursement only shops only reimburse you for a required purchase. A perfect example would be a dinner for two shop where they reimburse the purchase of two meals up to a certain amount. The second type of shop would be a set fee shop. This shop provides a set fee for completing the shop with no reimbursement. You will see these types of shops where a purchase is not required and, in some instances, where a purchase is required but there is just a set fee. For example, if you do a restaurant shop that has a set fee of $14 you will receive $14 no matter the amount you spend on your shop. There are also combination shops where you are provided a reimbursement for your purchase and a set fee. Some companies tell you what you must purchase, some give you a specific category (such as an alcoholic beverage of your choice), and some allow you to purchase anything you would like up to a certain amount.

The income you make from mystery shopping can vary greatly from month to month depending on the fees paid for each shop and the number of shops you conduct each month. Most companies pay through PayPal, so it is essential to have a PayPal account set up. There are a few companies that pay via direct deposit and a limited few that still pay via check.

PayPal is an American company that supports online money transfers. Mystery shopping companies pay PayPal a small fee to pay their shoppers electronically. You do not pay a fee to receive the money for your shops. You can transfer that money directly into your checking or savings account at no cost to you.

I use the PayPal app. You can also login to the PayPal website. I log in when I receive a payment and within a minute, I have transferred the money to my bank account. Your PayPal account is associated with your email address. You need to make sure you sign up with each mystery shopping company using your PayPal account email address.

When you conduct a mystery shop any purchase that is required is made up front and then you are later reimbursed for that purchase. The average time to receive payment for a mystery shop you conduct is anywhere from 3 weeks to 90 days depending upon the mystery shopping company. Each company has their own payment process and timeline. This timeline is stated in your Independent Contractor Agreement (ICA) which you sign when you sign up with the company. It is important to read this contract when you first sign up because it not only gives you payment information but also any restrictions place on you by the company. There are rare instances when you accept a shop and will receive tickets to the attraction up front. This will be specified in the shop information when you sign up for it. For example, if you accept a shop to an amusement park you may receive 6 tickets in advance to conduct the shop. In this instance you would not be required to purchase the tickets in advance. This is rare but does happen on some shops. I have attended shops at events, tourist attractions, and amusement parks where I have received tickets in advance.

In general, the more complicated a shop is the higher the fee you get paid. You get paid extra when you have long reports to fill out, have extensive narratives, or conduct a hidden camera mystery shop. This is not always the case but occurs most of the time. I have completed long reports before which I was only given a small fee. Some companies pay a bonus if you turn in your report early or on time.

Some shoppers choose not to do reimbursement only shops. I however enjoy these shops because I get to purchase many items for free. I will sometimes also take reimbursement only shops for products that I do not want or need but will give them as birthday or Christmas presents. Mystery shopping can be an excellent way to complete your Christmas shopping. I have also purchased wedding gifts doing mystery shopping. I also like reimbursement only shops because you get the opportunity to try new products as they come on the market free of charge.

There are some mystery shops where coupons or reward cards can be used. It is important to check the guidelines of the shop before you use these items to make sure they are allowed. There are some mystery shops that require you to use a coupon. When I conduct mystery shops that allow credit card use I either use my air miles or cash back card so I can get extras while mystery shopping.

I only take shops where I want or need something unless I am using the item as a gift. Then I take the money I would have spent on the gift and save it instead. This can be a great way to build up your savings account.